TEXT : HELENI FRANTZI, Archaeologist
TRANSLATION : HELEN ZIGADA, B.A.

ACROPOLIS ATHENS

PHOTOGRAPHS: G. VOUTSAS

ATHENS, 1970

THE ACROPOLIS OF ATHENS

The purest expression of a brilliant era, of a unique moment, as one might say, in the life of ancient Athens and ancient Greece in general, is found on the Acropolis of Athens with its buildings of the 5th century B.C., erected during the thirty-year leadership of the Athenian politician Pericles.

The rock dominated by the Acropolis, i.e. the citadel, as its name denotes, rises steep and distant from the surrounding hills. There is only on the western slope a natural passage facilitating access to the area of the Acropolis.

What the visitor of today sees on the site which had been the most sacred of all places of worship in Greece, is of course quite different from the picture contemplated by an Athenian of the Classical Age. The natural environment has changed and successive damages have considerably altered the site, so that the temples and other sanctuaries on the Acropolis do not present the same aspect in our times. The area, which was a sanctuary possessing an internal unity, was isolated from the rest of the city, and the high walls running along the edges of the rock contributed to this isolation. In Classical years the Acropolis was a pre-eminently enclosed sanctuary consisting of several completely independent buildings. Thus, when worshippers climbed on the Acropolis and stepped beyond the Propylaea, they found themselves in a totally different environment from that of the noisy city.

This was then the appearance of the Acropolis in Classical times. In much earlier times however, the Acropolis was a habitable area, i.e. it was both citadel and city, as revealed by excavations carried out on the site during the last century and later. There exist traces of habitation on the Acropolis, dating to the Early Helladic period, from 3500 to 3000 B.C., while excavations under the Propylaea uncovered wells also containing Early Helladic pottery. Life continued on the rock in later centuries till the Mycenaean times. The rock had so far no strong fortification; it seems that then, for the first time, apart from the houses, the palace of the Mycenaean king was built on the Acropolis. Excavations on the site place this palace on the location where the temple of Athena Polias was subsequently built, southwards of the Erechtheion. Ruins of the building itself are not preserved, and the only indication to its location is provided by the traces of a staircase, built of sandstone, which gave access to the palace. On the same area where the palace was built, were uncovered walls of houses contemporary to the palace.

However, when the Acropolis became the seat of the Mycenaean king, walls had to be built around the rock for greater protection against enemy attacks. Thus, in the second half of the 13th century (1250 - 1225 B.C.), a wall constructed of large irregular poros stones surrounded and protected the top of the rock. The walls of that period were named Cyclopean, for they were believed to have been built by the Cyclops. It is precisely this form, as encountered on the Athenian Acropolis in Mycenaean times, i.e. consisting of a palace of the Mycenaean sovereign and fortified walls built around the rock, that occurs also in the principal Mycenaean acropoleis of Mycenae, Tiryns, and Gla in Kopaïs. At that time there was no temple and no statue of a god on the Acropolis; the hearth was inside the Mycenaean palace. Near the palace, a sacred peribolos enclosed very old cults and signs, such as those of the trident of Poseidon, i.e. of the sea that had sprung from the rock when the god Poseidon had struck that spot with his trident, and of the olive tree which had suddenly grown when the goddess Athena had struck on the same place, during the dispute for supremacy of the one or the other deity over the city, according to tradition. This myth of course is later, but the signs were there since very old times. In later years the Erechtheion was built on that site and included all the cults.

The Mycenaean wall followed a continuous line; on the northwestern part of the rock and on a lower level, there was an extension of this wall. This extension has preserved its ancient name, known to us from Thucydides' narrative: it was named Pelargic. Within this extension of the wall on the flat top of the rock, there exist caverns which were dedicated in Classical times to Apollo, Olympian Zeus, and Pan.

Inside the walls of the Acropolis there was a water spring, the northern fountain, near the cavern of Aglauros, the mythical daughter of Cecrops worshipped since very old times like her sister Pandrosos; one could go down the wooden steps to draw water from the fountain. The existence of this water source within the fortification would certainly be an advantage in case of enemy invasion; the same scene is encountered in the corresponding acropoleis of Mycenae and Tiryns. Most probably one could descend to the northern fountain from the Acropolis at the point where the house of Arrhephoroi was later built (see below).

The main entrance to the Acropolis during Mycenaean times was on the western side, which was the only accessible way to the rock. In the beginnings of the 5th century, a marble propylon was built on the western side, and on the same location were also erected the great Propylaea of the Classical era.

Apart from the western entrance however, there were also two small gates on the northern side. The one was on the north-western descent leading to the caverns mentioned above; the other was situated near the site where the Erechtheion was later built. It seems that the latter had been used by the inhabitants of the Acropolis in cases of emergency, but it had not been preserved for a long time. Both these small gates of the northern side were not visible to the enemy standing outside the wall.

We have already mentioned the western entrance of Mycenaean times. In those years the south-western side of the entrance was protected by a bastion constructed on that site and surrounding a natural fortification point existing there. During Classical times the bastion was covered with poros stones and on it was erected the temple of Athena or Wingless Victory.

Certain sections of the wall from the Mycenaean fortification are still preserved, as uncovered by the careful excavations carried out on the rock. Thus we see parts of the wall preserved in front of the Propylaea, inside the Pinakotheke, near the north-western descent to the caverns, near the building of Arrhephoroi. Another discernible section of the wall is near the Erechtheion, from where we can follow it to the Acropolis Museum, in the south-western corner of the Parthenon, and finally southwards of the Propylaea. This latter part of the wall was the reason for the non-completion of the plan of the south wing of the Propylaea in Classical times.

The Mycenaean period is succeeded on the Helladic lands circa 1000 B.C. by a new era characterized by continuous migrations and settlements of new races in the various centres of Hellenism. This era is known by a great historical event, the descent of the Dorians, i.e. the new races coming from the North, bringing to the civilization of the Jonians and the Achaeans new, warlike, elements, since these people were warriors. While in Mycenaean times a small settlement was also formed under the Acropolis in addition to the houses which existed on it, inhabitants are once more concentrated around the rock. During these Dark Ages, called Geometric times, as long as the migrations of the Dorians lasted, nothing is very clear about the social and political life of Athens.

With the passing of time, however, the inhabitants come down from the Acropolis and form settlements in the plains. The first serious attempt to unite all these independent settlements into one city is attributed by Thucydides to Theseus, the son of Aegeus.

The enclosure surrounding the old cults continues to exist on the Acropolis, but at the same time altars were built and votive offerings presented to the gods. The old Mycenaean deity with its demonic hypostasis is slowly replaced by the twelve Olympian gods, although we know at present that many of these gods existed in Prehistoric times, too. Thus we have a survival of the old cult in later centuries.

The end of the Geometric era, which was the time of race migrations as we have already seen, coincides with the turn of the 7th to the 6th century. At the beginning of the new era which succeeds the Geometric and is named Archaic, the political form changes, too, in Greece. In all Hellenic centres there are no longer kings, while powerful political personalities, the tyrants, prevail. In Athens, from 594 till 560 B.C., Solon, one of the «Seven Wise Men» of ancient Greece, as well as a philosopher and a poet, brings about significant changes to the system of government. Towards the middle of the 6th century, he is succeeded by Peisistratus from Brauron, who remained in power till circa 520 B.C. Since Solon's time however, the first bases for democracy had already been laid, and so, when after Peisistratus' death his sons, the Peisistratides, took over, they were unable to remain in power for long. Towards the end of the 6th century B.C. Kleisthenes introduces the first democratic changes.

This was then the picture presented by the political life of Athens at the end of the Geometric and during the Archaic period. Already in the 7th century B.C. we note a new layout in the western entrance of the Acropolis. Excavations revealed sections of various walls constructed on that point apparently for the purpose of facilitating access to the western entrance. According to the latest investigation and study undertaken with respect to these walls of the western side, it appears that these formed the Enneapylon (Wall with nine gates) mentioned in ancient sources. Due to a confusion existing even in ancient times, the Enneapylon had been chronologically identified with the Pelargic, of which we have already spoken, i.e. it had been considered as a Mycenaean wall. At present, research rejects this chronological classification and considers the Enneapylon as belonging to the Geometric and Archaic times.

At the end of the 7th century B.C., on the site where the Parthenon was subsequently built, an ancient temple had been erected, whose signs are still preserved on the northern side of the Parthenon. This temple was named by the archaeologists who excavated it in the last century «Old Parthenon» (Urparthenon). It has a length of one hundred feet, it is therefore « Hekatompedos », as referred to by inscriptions. In Classical times the sekos of the Parthenon was « Hekatompedos ». According to studies made on the preserved architectural parts that must have belonged to this temple, the Old Parthenon had its eastern roof horizontal and its western apsidal. At this stage the temple must have had a pediment only on the eastern side: archaeologists who have studied the architectural remains, and especially the German archaeologist Buschor, ascribe to this side a poros pediment with representation of a lioness attacking a bull, an oriental motif existing since older times. Only half of the pediment is preserved, while the corresponding part, i.e. another lioness with a bull, has perished (Today this group is exhibited in the first Room of the Acropolis Museum). This poros pediment is chronologically classified to the first decade of the 6th century B.C.

From the second quarter of the 6th century B.C., there was another temple on the Acropolis, dedicated to the goddess Athena. Today we can only see the foundations of this temple, which was built of poros, just southwards of the Erechtheion. Part of the northern side of this temple was covered in Classical times by the Korai porch of the Erechtheion. According to the investigations carried out, the plan of the temple is restored as that of a Doric temple which was peripteral, i.e. it had all around Doric columns, six on the narrow sides and twelve on the long sides; the interior was rectangular in antis with internal colonnade. It consisted of three sections, typically recurring in almost all the temples of Ancient Greece: the entrance to the temple and the pronaos leading to the main naos, the sekos, were on the eastern side. The sekos was divided by a wall into two chambers, the eastern and the western, in a way that the two chambers did not communicate with each other. In the eastern chamber was the old wooden cult statue of the goddess (the «xoanon») which was believed to be « διϊπετές » (to have fallen from Zeus), i.e. to have fallen from heaven. The statue remained there until much later times, that is after the Erechtheion was built. Only as late as 406 B.C., was it transported from the old temple to the Erechtheion. The western chamber was destined for the worship of Erechtheus, the old priest of Athena and king of the land, whom the goddess welcomes maternally in her temple, as told by ancient tradition and particularly by Homer.

Inside the sekos a colonnade is restored in two rows with three columns in each row: it was thus divided into three parts (three aisles). The opisthodomos is on the narrow western side behind the sekos; one could enter it only from the west.

At this point we should note that many architectural problems arose during the study of this temple, due to lack of data for the safe restoration of its plan. It was originally thought that a poros temple existed consisting of the sekos and having no external columns. This temple was dated to 570 B.C. It was believed that the poros pediments, found along with other smaller ones and that of the lioness of the Old Parthenon (Urparthenon) during the excavations carried out on the Acropolis in the last century, belonged to that temple when it had its original form. According to measurements on the temple and the pediments, investigators attribute to this «old temple», as the temple of Athena Polias was named after an inscription of the 5th century B.C., two poros pediments, approximately 15 m. in length. On the one are depicted in the centre lions attacking a bull, while to the left and right are portrayed Herakles wrestling with Triton, and the Three-bodied demon; we can still discern the colours with which the pediment was painted. Two couchant lions are depicted in the centre of the other pediment, while from the ends two snakes writhe approaching each other.

Since the representation of this pediment has a more sacred character, it was considered to have belonged to the eastern side of the temple, whilst the pediment with Herakles etc., is attributed to the western side. At present they are in the Acropolis Museum. Later study of the pediments however, proved that the temple of Polias had been peripteral since the beginning, i.e. since 570 B.C. it had columns around all four sides.

Beside the pediments, other architectural members from the upper part of the «old temple» have been also preserved: the metopes which probably had a relief decoration on the eastern side only, those of the other sides being undecorated: fragments of a four-horse chariot and of Hermes with the pipe have been preserved, considered to have belonged to the metopes of the «old temple». The sima bearing an engraved and painted decoration and the acroteria with a Gorgon representation have also been preserved. Contrary to the rest of the temple and the poros pediments, these architectural parts were made of marble.

Towards the end of the 6th century, circa 520 B.C., the poros pediments were replaced by marble ones. On the eastern pediment Athena is portrayed attacking the giant Engelados, who has already sat on the ground. There are creeping giants on the corners, while between the central composition and the corners are preserved fragments of other god-giants (The pediment is exhibited in the Acropolis Museum after reconstruction and more detailed study of the figures on the various parts). What was decorating the western side of the temple is not exactly known.

At the same period, i.e. the 6th century B.C., other smaller buildings, most probably rectangular in form, existed on the Acropolis, but their location on the site is entirely unknown. From these buildings, which were not necessarily treasuries, the poros pediments and other architectural members are preserved. We have pediments from at least five buildings, now exhibited in the Acropolis Museum. They all belong to the beginning of the 6th century B.C., and they are still very influenced from the world of myth which dominated 7th century art. Hence the subjects depicted on the pediments are pre-eminently mythical. Among the pediments we note the representation of Troïlos and Achilles on the well known «pediment of the olive-tree», of Hydra, of Herakles fighting with the «ἅλιος γέρων» (old man of the sea), i.e. Nereus; also preserved, though not so well, are the two pediments of the procession and that of the « Deification of Herakles » which is dated to circa 560 - 550 B.C. These poros pediments had been painted and part of the colour is still preserved today.

These were the main buildings on the Acropolis during the 6th century B.C. In these buildings and in the free space between them, many votive offerings were erected, mostly statues presented to the goddess Athena and to the other gods. A number of these statues had pedestals with inscriptions showing the name of the dedicator and the god to whom the statue was dedicated. Many of these votive offerings have been preserved and are today exhibited in the Acropolis Museum. They portray young epheboi, riders, such as the famous « Rampin Horseman »—his body is in the Acropolis Museum and his head in the Louvre— various animals, and young maidens, the splendid Korai, a rich series of female statues with the characteristic dress falling on their body in exquisite folds. The Korai are often works of great artists, very few works of whose are preserved at present. The pedestals of some of the Korai have also been preserved, and so we know both the person who offered them and the artist who created them. It is not always certain, however, that a Kore belongs to the pedestal attributed to her. Thus a Kore is often conventionally named after the artist inscribed on the pedestal. At this point we may mention a great artist of approximately the end of the 6th century B.C., Antenor, to whom a Kore is ascribed, and the artist of Aristodikos (whose statue is in the National Museum) to whom another Kore is attributed (Inv. No. 673). We shall also mention the Kore of Euthydikos (Inv. No. 686) dating to the beginning of the 5th century B.C., named after the man who presented her. In all these statues the colours have been partly preserved.

At the end of the 6th century B.C. one could enter the Acropolis from a marble propylon which had in the meantime replaced the old Mycenaean entrance. It consisted of a gate having in front and at the back a row of columns supporting the roof. It was burned during the fire set by the Persians on the Acropolis to burn the sanctuaries, and was rebuilt some time later. The largest part of it was demolished when the Propylaea were erected on that site.

At the beginning of the 5th century a temple consecrated to the goddess Athena started being constructed on the location where the Parthenon was later built. The construction had reached a small height however, when the invasion of the Persians against Greece occurred. All the sanctuaries on the Acropolis were burnt, and the Mycenaean wall suffered severe damages. The temple of Athena Polias was destroyed; it was the only one to be rebuilt after the victorious end of the wars of the Greeks against the Persians, to house the wooden statue of the goddess which the Athenians had taken with them on their ships when they had left their city.

After the end of the war with the victory of the Greeks over the Persians, following the naval battle of Salamis and the battle of Plataea in 479 B.C., some sanctuaries on the Acropolis were temporarily repaired; apart from the « old temple », it seems that the Athenians tried to restore the temple lying under the Parthenon. As already mentioned above, the propylon on the western side was rebuilt and the Acropolis was fortified again. On the northern side of the wall, according to tradition, Themistocles had certain sections and architectural parts of the ruined temples built into the wall, so that Athenians would not forget the fact that the united Greeks had brought defeat on the fantastically greater number of their enemies. The wall was constructed of rectangular poros stones, and, according to tradition, was finished by Kimon, who completed the southern section after the victory of the river Eurymedon in 467 B.C. The votive offerings that had escaped destruction, even those in pieces, were hidden by the Athenians in the clefts of the rock, where they remained protected, just as they had been buried, till the last century, when they were again brought to light through the systematic excavations undertaken.

For the rest of the area however, an oath had been taken never to rebuild the sanctuaries, but to leave the site just as it was, as a perpetual image of the destruction and sacrilege suffered by the most sacred place of Greece. Fortunately this decision was altered, and some time later, after the battle of Plataea and before the beginning of the Peloponnesian War, a great constructive activity began, as a result of which the sanctuaries were rebuilt on the Acropolis. The rock then took on a new appearance that remained essentially unchanged in later centuries, except, of course, for the inevitable natural or barbaric damages. The reconstruction of the sanctuaries was not an isolated event in the life of ancient Athens. In the years after the Median wars, great figures dominated the political and artistic world. On the one hand we have the political mind of Pericles, the « one man statesmanship », and on the other hand the many-sided personality of Pheidias, the main organizer of all the artistic creations. Thus the plans of the mind are realized on the site by the great artist with the warm support of the statesman.

Under his title of elected general, Pericles had proposed the convocation of an artistic committee which would take decisions for the construction of sanctuaries on the Acropolis. Pericles himself was a member of that committee and used to discuss all problems with Pheidias. It was then proposed to erect a great temple in honour of Athena, the patroness of the city; in that temple — which constituted rather an evidence of the wealth and power achieved by Athenian democracy— the goddess would be worshipped as Athena Parthenos. It was also decided to build the Propylaea in monumental form, the Erechtheion, where the old cult statue of Athena Polias would be transferred from the «old temple», and the temple of Athena or Wingless Victory. The construction of the Parthenon began first, followed by that of the Propylaea. In the meantime however, the destructive Peloponnesian War had started, which somehow delayed the completion of the works on the Acropolis. During the peace intervals of the war, the Erechtheion and the temple of Athena Nike were built.

THE PROPYLAEA

We have already mentioned that the main entrance to the Acropolis was situated since Mycenaean times on the western side. At the beginning of the 5th century a marble propylon in antis with North-East orientation was erected on the location of the Mycenaean gate, and was subsequently covered in great part by the Classical Propylaea; only a small section is preserved today at the south - eastern corner of the Propylaea.

The Acropolis could be approached by a path leading from the southern slope, continuing on the western slope, meeting the procession way of the Panathenaea, past the bastion with the temple of Wingless Victory, and on to the northern end of the western slope, where in Hellenistic times a pedestal was set up with a four-horse chariot led by a hero of the Hellenistic period, later —after 20 B.C. —replaced by a quadriga led by Agrippa, Augustus' son in law (The monument on that pedestal, no longer preserved today, is called Agrippa's Monument). From that point the path turned southwards, reached as far as the bastion of Nike, then continued towards the central entrance of the Propylaea.

In the 1st century A.D. the path was covered by a wide baroque stairway in the fashion of the Roman period, which however had not been preserved over a long time. In front of this stairway a gate flanked by two towers was constructed in later times, forming part of the fortification built around the Acropolis. The gate was named Beulé Gate, after the French archaeologist who discovered it, and had been built with the re-used material of older monuments. The towers were older than the Gate.

The Propylaea constituted a porch before entering into the sacred area of the Acropolis, isolating the worshippers from the outside world. We can discern a central building and two wings to the right and left of it, oriented northwards and southwards. Mnesicles was the architect of the building; construction works lasted from 437 to 432 B.C., and were interrupted by the Peloponnesian War. The material used in this monumental structure was marble; the earlier Propylon was also constructed of marble. Low steps led to the western facade where six Doric columns supported the roof with the architrave, frieze and cornice, forming a facade of Doric temple. The columns stood on a raised platform of four steps, while on the eastern facade there were corresponding columns standing directly on the rock; thus the eastern side of the Propylaea is on a higher level, and the roof of the eastern porch is higher than that of the western, while both are crowned with pediments. The carved panels, the cofferings of the ceiling, were of marble, exquisitely decorated and painted with gilt rosettes or stars in the centre.

The cross - wall used as pylon was built on the side of the eastern porch. It was erected on a flight of five steps and had five doors, the one in the centre being the largest, and the two at the side -ends being the smallest. Usually only the smaller doors were open, while the middle one was opened only on festive days to allow passage, on the path crossing the entire middle section of the Propylaea, to the worshippers and the animals that would be sacrificed on the altars. We should also note that of the two porches, the western had a greater length than the eastern, while their width was the same. This great length however necessitated internal supports; hence, to the left and right of the central doorway, three Ionic columns were placed on either side. The Ionic style was preferred here, for Ionic columns are more slender and the whole area thus presents a certain elevation which the Doric columns would not have given it. The Ionic capitals were coloured, matching with the cofferings and the dark Eleusinian stone that had been used on the lintels, orthostatai, benches, etc. As tradition tells us, there were votive offerings on the whole area; among these were the statues of Hermes Propylaios of Alcamenes and the Charites of Socrates.

As already stated, there are two wings to the right and left of the central building of the Propylaea; the one has an entrance to the North and the other to the South. The north wing stands on a poros platform; it is the Pinakotheke (cf. Pausanias' description), which had on the southern side three Doric columns between antae. The first room, the prodomos, was closed behind by a wall which had a door to communicate with the back chamber and two windows to the right and left. In the main chamber the wall was decorated at the height of the windows with a band of dark Eleusinian stone; it is probably there that hang the pictures of which Pausanias speaks when describing the buildings of the Acropolis in the 2nd century A.D. However, no evidence of these pictures has been preserved inside the building; even the walls had not been smoothed to receive the pictures. From this side a stair led to a water spring of the Classical period, the Klepsydra, known in ancient times as Empedo.

The south wing also had three Doric columns between antae, but one could not advance from the prodomos into the main chamber as in the Pinakotheke. The wall here had neither door nor windows and did not reach to the western side where the one anta stood: it stopped behind the third column. While the western side of the Pinakotheke was closed with a wall, at the south wing the space behind the anta remained free. Two reasons explain why no chamber had been built behind the pro-domos, and why the western side of the south wing had remained open: at the eastern end in front of the south wing, there was a remaining section of the Mycenaean wall, and a room built behind the prodomos would have covered part of it. Yet the western side remained incomplete for another important reason. At the western end, on the bastion which had covered part of the rock since older times as already mentioned above, stood the temple of Wingless Victory. It would have been therefore difficult to close the western side of the room at this point and erect a wall that would have somehow isolated the temple.

On the eastern side of both wings a porch was also planned that would open eastwards with internal and external colonnade. The plan was not carried out for the Peloponnesian War had started in the mean-time; however, there would have been an additional difficulty, at least for the construction of the southern porch: on the southern side stood the sanctuary of Artemis Brauroneia, and if the porch were constructed it would have partly covered the sanctuary, a thing that would have been certainly considered undesirable by the priests of the Brauroneion. Another fact indicates that the plan of the Propylaea had not been completed: on the outer surface of the walls the square projections (ancones) had not been removed; they can still be seen today. These remained until the last stage of the construction works and were removed only when the building was finished.

In later years the Propylaea underwent some changes in their plan, especially during the Frankish occupation, when a high tower was built next to them. This tower remained until the last century, when it was demolished, so that the Acropolis would take on again its old appearance.

In 1656 the central part of the Propylaea was struck by lightning which exploded the gun-powder stocked there by the Turk Yousouf Aga; thus the middle section was irreparably destroyed.

THE TEMPLE OF ATHENA NIKE

The temple of « Apteros Nike » (Wingless Victory) was constructed on the bastion which was built in Mycenaean times and had ever since surrounded the rock on the western side of the Acropolis as a natural fort. On a lower level have been found fragments of an altar, or altars, that had been there since the middle of the 6th century B.C., as denoted by an inscription found *in situ*; there was also a section of a peribolos from an open sanctuary, probably dating, along with one of the altars, to the beginnings of the 5th century B.C. In Classical times the bastion was faced with poros in the isodomic technique. On its western side there are two conches, most probably used for cult purposes.

This bastion is also connected with the myth of Aegeus, who, according to tradition, had jumped off the rock at that point, when he saw his son Theseus sailing back on a ship with black sails. The sanctuary of Aegeus is below that bastion.

An inscription has been preserved since 448 B.C., stating that in honour of Athena Nike a temple would be built on the bastion and an altar erected and a priestess of Athena appointed. The temple was built according to plans by Kallikrates, the collaborator of Iktinos on the Parthenon. Eventually the execution of the plan was postponed due to the interference of the Peloponnesian War, and only in 427 B.C., did the construction of the charming little temple of Athena begin. Its construction lasted from 427 to 424 B.C. It appears however, that in the period between 448 and 427 B.C. another similar small temple was built by the river Ilisos, probably the Metroon at Agrae, completely ruined at present.

The temple of Athena Nike was built after the completion of the Propylaea. The ground level on which the temple and altar were erected had been paved with slabs. The temple was accessible from the south wing of the Propylaea, or from a small stair on the northern side of the bastion encountered on the way from the path of the Propylaea.

The temple was constructed of Pentelic marble and was tetrastyle amphiprostyle, i.e. it had four columns of the Ionic style on both the eastern and western sides. It consists only of a sekos which has no wall on the eastern side; there are only two pillars between the antae at the ends of the northern and southern side. The antae were joined with the pillars by a lattice. In contrast, on the western side there is no opening; there are only antae at the two ends of the wall. In the sekos was the wooden cult statue of Athena, the xoanon, holding in the right hand a pomegranate and in the left the helmet.

Above the architrave, which consisted of three projecting fasciae, there was a frieze decorated on the eastern side with a representation

16

of the Assembly of gods (we can still see *in situ* the frieze slabs of that side), while on the other sides it was decorated with scenes from the battles of the Greeks among themselves or against the Persians, and especially scenes from the battle of Plataea in 479 B.C.; some plaster reproductions are on the southern side, while the originals are in the British Museum. The representations on the pediments have not been preserved.

At the end of the 5th century B.C., a parapet was raised around the temple to protect the free sides (northern, western and southern); it consisted of marble slabs of 1 m. height, having sculptured representations on the outside, and starting from the point where the stair was on the northern side. The marble slabs are today in the Acropolis Museum. Winged Victories are depicted setting up trophies and leading sacrificial oxen, while the goddess Athena is seated on a rock nearby. The slabs of this parapet are of a later date than the frieze of the temple, which, too, is of a later date than the Parthenon. In any case, the depicted Nikai possess an unsurpassed gracefulness, as they are represented in their everyday activities with such light liveliness that one would imagine them stepping out of their frames and advancing on the space of the Acropolis.

In 1686 the Turks pulled the temple down completely to build with its material on the Propylaea a battery which was dismantled just after the liberation, in 1835. The temple was immediately re-erected (1836 - 1843), but in 1935 it had to be reconstructed again from its foundations (1935 - 1939); it was then that were uncovered the older altar and sacred peribolos mentioned above.

On entering the Acropolis from the Propylaea and leaving behind the temple of Athena Nike, one comes across some small sanctuaries, only the foundations of which are preserved today. At the south-western corner of the rock, before the temple of Nike, is the sanctuary of Artemis Brauroneia with its sacred peribolos. It is known that the cult of Artemis was brought on the Acropolis by Peisistratus in the 6th century from his homeland Brauron, but the sanctuary was rebuilt after the Persian Wars. There were colonnades on the southern and eastern side. Further to the east, there was another building referred to in inscriptions as the Chalkotheke, where the bronze votive offerings (weapons and other accessories) were being kept. One could enter the Chalkotheke from a propylon on the northern side of a buttress supporting the terrace of the Parthenon. The propylon led to a court and thence to the Chalkotheke.

On the northern side of the Acropolis, westwards of the Erechtheion, there was a small building with a porch and an adjoining court. Pausanias calls it the building of Arrhephoroi; the Arrhephoroi were young girls, aged 7 - 11, at the service of the goddess Athena. From the adjoining court the girls descended from the rock to the location where the sanctuary of Eros and Aphrodite stood, bringing there or taking from there various covered objects.

Still further to the west were the quarters of the priestess of Athena, consisting of two rooms and a porch.

The sanctuaries seen to the right and left of the Propylaea were built on different levels with courts in the intervening space. There was a large court at the back of the Propylaea, and at the court end on the eastern side, on a special high pedestal, stood the statue of Athena Promachos, made by Pheidias in 445 B.C. from the spoils of Marathon. The pedestal rested on the western wall of the terrace of the « old temple » (of Athena Polias); this wall, of which only the foundations survived, was the old Mycenaean wall used as buttress for the Mycenaean palace.

From the pedestal of the Promachos is preserved today a part of the base cornice decorated with an Ionic cymatium. The statue itself was taken by Justinian to Constantinople, where it was destroyed in 1204 by the population (as reported by Niketas Choniates). In the same court there were also many other votive statues. We should mention another work of Pheidias, the statue of Athena Lemnia, presented on the Acropolis by the Athenian colonizers sent on the island of Lemnos between 451 and 448 B.C.

THE PARTHENON

On advancing southwards from this court with the votive offerings, one reaches a small propylon, which provides entrance into another court, as mentioned above. On its eastern side, the court had steps for the ascent to the terrace of the Parthenon. For the construction of this great temple, elements of the Ionic style were superbly combined to those of a Doric temple. Except for the western side, the walls of the sekos, as well as the whole roof, were destroyed in 1687, when the gunpowder stored by the Turks in the Parthenon exploded during the siege of the Acropolis by Morosini. Part of the pediments were also destroyed at that time. The Parthenon was the first building erected by the Athenians on the Acropolis after the Persian invasion. An enormous sum was necessitated for its construction, which would have been impossible to raise, had the money from the treasury of the Allies not been used for that purpose. When in 454 B.C., the treasury of the Allies was transferred from Delos to the Acropolis, 1/60 of each talent was set aside to be used for the building of the temple.

The Parthenon was constructed between the years 447-438 B.C. by the most famous architect of the time, Iktinos, with Kallikrates as his assistant. The temple was peripteral amphiprostyle. It was consecrated in 438 B.C., when the great chryselephantine (gold and ivory) statue of Athena made by Pheidias was also consecrated. The sculpture decoration of the temple however was not completed, and it was only in 432 B.C. that the work was ended after the pediments had been finished. We know about the architecture of the temple from the Roman writer Vitruvius, who records that Iktinos had written a book on the Parthenon.

The temple was built on the site of the Old Parthenon (Urparthenon) and the other Pre-Periclean temple whose construction had only reached a small height at the beginnings of the 5th century B.C. On the northern side it was founded on bedrock, whereas on the southern side an artificial platform, on which the temple stood, was constructed in considerable depth, for the rock on that side is fairly lower. The crepidoma forming the foundation of the temple consists of three high steps. On the lower step the dimensions are 72.53×33.88 m. On the narrow sides which provided access to the temple, there were supplementary small marble steps to facilitate ascent. On the higher step of the crepidoma, the stylobate, stand the columns surrounding the sekos, 8 on the narrow and 17 on the long sides, according to the classical conception of the ratio of the long to the narrow sides of a temple. The columns are Doric; they have no base but stand directly on the stylobate. Whilst on the lower part they are wide, they become narrower on the way up, having a greater width at about 2/5 of their height (the so-called entasis). Entrance was on the eastern side, where the pronaos was, with six columns between antae. The opisthodomos had a similar arrangement. From the eastern side one stepped through a door into the sekos, where the cult statue of Athena stood. As already stated, the sekos had a length of one hundred feet. Both the pteron, i.e. the outer colonnade, and the sekos had a roof with carved panels, the cofferings, of which we have already spoken when describing the Propylaea. In the sekos, the cofferings were of wood. A wall separated the main sekos with the cult statue from another chamber situated further to the west; one could enter it from the western side, where the opisthodomos was. Inside the sekos, whose walls had no opening, there was a colonnade in two rows with ten columns in each, dividing the area into three parts. Near the western wall of the sekos there was another row of three columns running parallel to the wall and forming a Π-shape with the columns of the long sides. The statue stood on the axis of the sekos; for its protection a balustrade was placed between the columns and panels in front of it. The columns separating the middle aisle from the side aisles were in two tiers separated from each other by an architrave. Thus the colonnade was, as we say, superimposed.

Light was coming in from the eastern side through the opening of the door and one light-well. In the western room there were four Ionic columns; the name of « Parthenon » was given to that room, but it is not exactly known what it was used for. On the contrary, we do know that the treasure of the temple was kept in the opisthodomos. In Christian times (6th century A.D.), when the Parthenon was converted into a church, an apse was built on the eastern side, the sanctuary apse, while doors were opened on the wall separating the sekos from the western room. Moreover, in the western room the walls were painted over with hagiographies, part of which can be still seen today.

This great temple has been mostly admired for the proportions existing between all its architectural parts: the ratio of the diameter to the height of the column is 1: 5.5, of the diameter to the distance between two columns is 1: 2.25. In general this proportion is expressed by the ratio of the proportions to each other, which is 4:9. On the basis of this ratio the Parthenon, contrary to the other Doric temples of Greece, is the first one to have 8 columns on its narrow sides and 17 on its long, whereas all Doric temples till that time had 6 columns on their narrow sides.

Apart from these proportions and the ratio existing between the various architectural elements, there is another feature which gives the temple a more harmonious and classical appearance. These are the various deviations from the straight line, observed in the various parts. Thus on the crepidoma, the upper surface deviates from the straight line and forms a small curvature, and so does the interior floor of the temple. The same curvature is noted in the upper part of the temple in the architrave. On the other hand, the columns are inclined inwards, and so are the walls of the sekos. A counter inclination, i.e. outwards, is observed in the upper part of the temple in the geison.

The Parthenon is admired not only as a perfect architectural structure, but also as a unique monument for the sculpture decorating it. The upper part of the temple, the entablature, consisting of the architrave, the frieze and the geison, was all covered with sculptured decoration. Only the architrave was undecorated, but while there were no sculptures on it, its eastern side was adorned with 26 Persian armours presented by Alexander the Great on the Acropolis after the battle of Granicus; an honorary inscription in gold letters for Nero was also added later. In the frieze, consisting of the triglyphs and the metopes, the decoration was made on the metope slabs. From the total number of

92 metopes, a part has been lost, another part is in foreign Museums; and 41 remain *in situ* on the monument, though badly damaged. These were the first sculptures produced to decorate the Parthenon; their making began in 447 and until 440 they were set in place. On each side is depicted a separate subject, but each scene may be depicted on more than one metope, as is the case on the northern side. On the eastern side was depicted the Gigantomachy with Athena as dominating figure; on the western side, the Amazonomachy; on the northern side, the sack of Troy with Menelaus and Helen (as they can be recognized) and Helios and Selene at the ends to the right and left; and on the southern side, where the metopes are best preserved, the Centauromachy. From the latter, a metope is preserved almost intact on the south-western corner of the building. The sculptured slabs of the metopes are still in their place on the eastern, western and northern sides. Those of the southern side are in the British Museum.

The differences in style among the various metopes are due to the fact that many artists had worked on them simultaneously; consequently the sculptures present both Archaic and later elements. Of course, Pheidias was the general supervisor for this work too, a fact which becomes apparent in the general principles followed in the art of these sculptures, constituting a new conception mainly expressed in the way the body is formed independent of details. Pheidias, however, was giving the direction to the work leaving the execution to his pupils. Perhaps he was himself preparing the sketches for the subjects with which the metopes would be decorated and the other artists worked on these. The metope slabs as well as the triglyphs were coloured and this gave life to the carved surface. The statues themselves, of course, remained white, but the triglyphs had a blue and the metopes a red background.

The band crowning the upper part of the triglyphs and metopes has an astragal decoration; above it begins the geison which consists of the horizontal and the two raking sides. These include on the narrow sides the sculptures of the pediments made from 438-7 till 433-2 B.C. From the marble sculptures, which are carved almost in the round, very few survive; the greater part of the east pediment has been mostly damaged. Some of its figures however have survived and are now in the British Museum. On the east pediment was depicted the birth of Athena in the presence of the other Olympian gods. The spectator may easily imagine the preceding scene, i.e. all the gods assembled and watching in astonishment Athena being born from the head of Zeus. While the gathering of gods is concentrated for a moment in the centre where this amazing event occurs, it is then dispersed towards the sides.

In the centre stood Athena in full armour next to Zeus seated on his throne, while Hephaistus watches the scene in surprise. To the left

21

of Zeus stood Hera, and further to the left Iris, related to the group of Demeter and Kore who are seated. Dionysus is seated near the end; he does not look towards the centre but towards the corner where Helios (the Sun) rises. Similarly on the other end of the pediment the seated figures of the gods look towards Selene (the Moon) who is setting.

On the west pediment is represented the contest of Poseidon and Athena for the domination of the one or the other over the city of Athens. In the centre are portrayed Athena with the olive-tree and Poseidon with the trident; the chariots of the two gods are depicted on the sides as well as the heroes of the city. We can still see *in situ* on the northern corner of the pediment the group of Cecrops with one of his daughters.

Of the two pediments the western one should be of a later date; the figures here present greater movement, but this is natural, since in all temples, as a rule, the eastern pediment is more Archaic than the western, except for rare instances. In the composition of both however, the complex personality of Pheidias is again recognized, although here, too, the various figures could have been worked by several artists.

The same problem encountered in the metopes and the pediments also exists in the frieze which surrounds the upper part of the sekos inside the colonnade and has a continuous length of 160 m. and a height of 1 m. It is the first time that a frieze is seen on a Doric temple, for this element is purely Ionic. Here too a number of artists had worked on the figures, hence certain differences are discernible in the composition. Yet again there is certainly a general direction dominating the entire work, which was given by one artist, the «surveyor general», Pheidias.

The subject of the frieze is the procession of the Panathenaea, a festival established already in 566 B.C. by Peisistratus, and celebrated since then every four years as the Great Panathenaea. The procession starts from the south - western corner of the temple (where the frieze slabs are still *in situ*) and it is continued on the two long sides. The representation includes epheboi riders and other youths leading the sacrificial animals, elder demotes, chariots with apobats, etc. In total there were apart from the 12 gods, the heroes of the ten tribes and over 300 persons leading about 200 sacrificial animals. The procession ends on the eastern side of the temple, where the peplos is presented to Athena, at the centre of the frieze. To the right and left is the Assembly of gods (on the right: Athena, Hephaistus, Poseidon, Apollo, Artemis, Aphrodite and Eros; on the left: Zeus, Hera and Iris, Ares, Demeter, Dionysus, Hermes). At the ends stand the heroes of the ten tribes. The slabs of the frieze, on which these figures were carved, had a blue colour. The astounding composition and work of the frieze reaching to such perfection is admirable, although at the height it was placed

22

without being sufficiently lighted, no one could fully enjoy the imposing procession. A great part of the frieze is in the British Museum today, and one of the finest panels, on which one may recognize the hand of Pheidias himself, is in the Louvre.

There was a polychromy in the various ornaments and architectural parts of the temple but not in the main architectural features. The architects gave vivid colours, blue, red, gold, to the details and especially to the ornaments of the roof; we have already mentioned the coffered ceiling not only in the Parthenon, but also in the Propylaea and the Erechtheion, of which we shall speak later.

Terminating with the architectural reliefs decorating the Parthenon, we should also mention the painted acroteria at the two ends and in the middle of the narrow sides, consisting of palmette motifs of over 2 m. height. At each of the four ends of the roof there was a lion head, a false sima which was not pierced, and on the long sides over the geison covering tiles in floral shape.

We still have to speak about the great cult statue of Athena, standing in the sekos of the Parthenon. This statue was taken to Constantinople in the 5th century A.D., where it was destroyed. Today in the sekos a rectangular space of poros can be seen, on which stood the base of the statue having a height of 1.20 m. The statue and the base had a total height of approximately 12 m. The statue was worked by Pheidias from the time when the Parthenon started being built, i.e. from 447 B.C., and it was finished and placed in the sekos in 438 B.C. Today copies exist either in marble statues or in small sculpture works, giving a faint idea of what the statue must have been, as the traveller Pausanias described it in the 2nd century A.D. One of the copies, the marble «Varvakeion Athena», is in the National Museum, Athens.

Athena stood on the pedestal in frontal attitude slightly turned to the right. The statue was of wood covered with a chiton in gold leaf, which could be removed. On her chest was the aegis and on her head she was wearing the Attic helmet. She was leaning on the right leg, while the left, bent in the knee, was placed a little backwards. With the left hand she was resting on the shield, and on the same side was a long spear; on the right hand she was carrying a Nike of approximately 2 m. height, supported on a stele, at least as it appears in the copy of the « Varvakeion Athena ». The shield had on the inner surface a painted Gigantomachy and on the outer surface a relief representation of an Amazonomachy. Between the shield and Athena was the snake, the « household serpent » of the goddess. The face and other uncovered parts of the body were made of ivory; her attire was adorned with bracelets, earings and necklaces. On her sandals there was a relief representation of a Centauromachy. Also decorated was the front side of the base on which the statue stood:

the assembled gods were depicted watching the birth of Pandora. At the two ends of the base, Helios and Selene were portrayed. It is known that Pheidias was accused by his rivals of embezzling the gold for the dress of the goddess; he was brought to trial for that, but the accusation was never proved.

THE ERECHTHEION

The Erechtheion was built during the time of the Peloponnesian War on the northern side of the Acropolis opposite to the Parthenon, in order to include the wooden statue of Athena till then housed in the ancient temple of Polias. It was at this time that a section of the southern porch of the Erechtheion overlay a small part of the « old temple ».

The construction of the Erechtheion began in 421 B.C., but work was interrupted for a while during the Peloponnesian War to be resumed in 409 till 406 B.C., when it finally came to an end. On a building inscription of 409-8 B.C. the temple is referred to as «ὁ ναὸς ὁ ἐν πόλει ἐν ᾧ τὸ ἀρχαῖον ἄγαλμα» («the naos in the city, in which is the ancient statue»). The architect of the building however is not known but for the last period of construction: Philocles is cited as the architect in the accounts kept annually to inform the people of the expenses. Anyhow, it was assumed by many that the Erechtheion was also a work of Mnesicles. In Roman times certain parts of the Erechtheion were destroyed by fire and some alterations were made because of that.

The whole building presents many architectural problems due in great part to the fact that there were old cults and sacred signs on the site which had to be architecturally included in a single structure. Another reason has contributed, though not so substantially as the forementioned one, to the unusual design of the Erechtheion: the ground on which the structure was erected is not level on the whole surface, for the rock slopes downwards on the western side.

The sekos was on the eastern side and contained the wooden statue of the goddess. It is accessible through a prostyle pronaos with six Ionic columns of 6 m. height standing on a three-stepped crepidoma. We observe that neither the entasis nor the curvatures, espesially noted in the Parthenon, are present in the Ionic style; there is only an inclination of the columns towards the centre or inwards. Their upper part bears a lavish floral decoration in relief of anthemia and lotuses surrounded by an astragal; the capitals are also profusely decorated. The northernmost column is now in London. The columns support the entablature with the architrave consisting of three fasciae and the frieze in dark Eleusinian stone running on all four sides of the building and bearing representations from the myth of Erichthonios and other scenes in which some recognize the birth of Athena etc.; the figures in white marble are affixed on the Eleusinian stone. Some of the slabs are in the Acropolis Museum. It appears that there were no statues on the pediments.

Behind the porch with the columns is the wall of the sekos with a door in the centre and a window on either side. On the upper part of the wall we find again a rich decoration of anthemia and lotuses, an astragal surrounding an Ionic cymatium and further up a Lesbian cymatium with heart-shaped leaves. In the sekos was the « xoanon » of Athena, who was portrayed seated holding a phiale and dressed in the peplos offered to her by the Athenians during the Panathenaea festival. In front of the « xoanon » burned a gold lamp with a bronze palm-tree. The lamp with the palm-tree is ascribed by tradition to Callimachus. In the 6th century A.D., the eastern side of the Erechtheion was converted into a Christian church.

The western wall of the sekos rose from North to South without any opening, thus completely separating the eastern from the western section of the Erechtheion. We have therefore a double building, just as described by the traveller Pausanias, i.e. two adjacent areas, the one used for the worship of Athena and the other for the worship of Erechtheus, after whom the whole building was named. The western section had entrances on the North, West and South. Pausanias begins his description of the Erechtheion from the northern entrance. Today this is accessible through a wide stairway located near the eastern side of the building and leading to a paved court. On the western end of the northern side there was an entrance with a porch of six Ionic columns, four on a sigle line and one behind each of those at the angles. These columns with their exquisite decoration, a brilliant specimen of the Ionic style, were crowned by the entablature with the frieze which adorned the three sides of the northern porch. The space between the columns and the wall of the North entrance was roofed and on the ceiling were cofferings with superb decoration. On the marble floor of this stoa, on the eastern side, we notice that some slabs are missing; these would be also missing in ancient times, since Pausanias already relates that on this point was the mark from Poseidon's trident, or, according to an earlier tradition, the mark of Zeus' thunderbolt which struck Erechtheus. This mark can be seen even today. Exactly above this spot there is a gap in the roof, too, which signifies that this space was sacred and had to remain as it was. Above the marks of the trident, Pausanias records the altar of Hypatos Zeus, while the forementioned inscription of 409-8

B.C. cites the altar of Thyechoos, who was identified with Hypatos Zeus.

At the back of the porch was the wall with the great northern gate which had a sumptuous and imposing decoration: rosettes were carved on the marble frame while a magnificent decoration of anthemia and lotuses adorned the upper part. Today we see the restoration of the Roman and subsequent periods. The gate was leading to the areas of the western section of the Erechtheion. At the western end of the wall was another small door leading to the open sanctuary of Pandrosos, the daughter of Cecrops, who had her own precinct; there stood the altar of Herkeios Zeus and there grew the olive, the sacred tree of Athena, which was apparenly the sacred tree of Erechtheus or of Cecrops too, before becoming associated with the name of the goddess.

From the great gate one enters into the westernmost chamber of the whole western section, where was the Erechtheis sea, a well, as recorded by Pausanias, on the site of the water source that sprang when Poseidon struck the ground with his trident during his dispute with Athena over the naming of the city after the one or the other deity. It is characteristic however, that the sea was named Erechtheis, although it had been already attributed to Poseidon. For Erechtheus was also identified with Poseidon, since they were both Prehistoric deities related to the earth, before Poseidon became connected with the sea. There is another evidence of the Poseidon - Erechtheus relation: Pausanias mentions three altars inside the Erechtheion, i.e. that of Hephaistus, of the hero Boutes, and of Poseidon; this last altar was common for Erechtheus as well. In remote Prehistoric times both Poseidon and Erechtheus were Pre - Hellenic chthonic deities with a common cult. These altars were bothroi or eschares, situated in the easternmost chamber of the western compound, which was separated from the first chamber (westernmost) by a cross-wall not reaching to the ceiling of the building. There lay also the grave of Erechtheus who was worshipped in the form of the bevenolent serpent (οἰκουρὸς ὄφις). In historic times the snake connected Athena to Erechtheus and became the goddess' attendant. The chamber where Erechtheus was worshipped was probably divided into two parts, though this has not been absolutely ascertained.

On the western facade of the Erechtheion there is a wall not of the full height of the building on which stand four Ionic engaged columns between antae. The openings between the engaged columns were closed on the lower part by a built parapet and on the upper part by wooden railings (δρύφαxτα), with the exception of the last opening to the South, which had no railing. In Roman times the openings between the engaged columns were built and the railings became windows. On the western wall there was a small door providing access to the Pandroseion.

26

The peculiarity observed in the western side of the Erechtheion, i.e. the wall reaching a certain height and then continuing with engaged columns, is mainly explained by the chthonic character of the entire building: as the cult was performed in the presence of the people and sacrifices were offered on the altars existing there, it was necessary to have an opening to let light in and smoke from the sacrifices out.

The western wall of the Erechtheion meets the southern. At the south - western corner the building inscription of the Erechtheion, dating to 409-8 B.C., mentions the grave of Cecrops, the mythical king considered along with Erechtheus as the founder - hero of Athens. It seems that the grave was actually there, as it becomes also evident from the architectural peculiarity of the south - western corner. The grave extended under the porch of the Korai situated at the western end of the southern wall, and was surrounded by a temenos. The Korai porch stands on a high podium and is undoubtedly connected with the grave of Cecrops, just as this architectural form of above - ground structures over graves can be seen in other instances as well. The porch is not structurally connected with the rest of the Erechtheion. Its roof has not the same height as that of the rest of the building; also there is no frieze as in the remaining building. It was therefore constructed in order to cover the grave of Cecrops which lies on a lower level; one could descend to it by a stair at the eastern side of the porch. There was also a small door on the southern wall leading to the grave.

Behind the porch the wall had a row of orthostatai on the lower part, and was continued above in marble. On the upper part it had the refined rich and beautiful relief decoration of anthemia and lotuses as encountered on the upper part of the wall running on all four sides of the building.

Let us now come to the celebrated Korai porch. It had already been completed during the first stage of construction of the Erechtheion. On the pedestal, which formed, as already stated, an above - ground structure over the grave of Cecrops, six Korai, the Caryatides, wearing the girded Doric peplos, support the roof of the building in the place of columns. Four of the Korai stand in a single line and the two are behind those placed at either corner of the first row. The second Kore from the left (of the first row) is in the British Museum; its plaster reproduction is seen on the monument. On their heads they carry the capital adorned with relief decoration, and their hair falls abundant on their back. The left hand holds the himation. They stand bending the knee of the leg which is towards the centre. It is characteristic that the frieze is missing in the Korai porch, an element whose importance we have already stressed as denoting the lack of connection of the porch to the rest of the Erechtheion.

It has become customary today to call the six Korai « Caryatides », though they do not portray women from Caryai. Besides, the building inscription of 409-8 B.C. refers to them as « Korai ». In any case, it is evident that they were not all made by one artist. As we see them, leaning on one leg, with their chiton falling in folds according to the stance or the bent knee, they do not give the impression of carrying the weight of a whole roof, but rather of just standing there, on the edge of the building, contemplating the sacred area with all the grace and freshness of young maidens.

As we have already seen, the plan of the Erechtheion satisfied certain needs and included sacred signs and very old cults performed here on this part of the rock. Its plan therefore is not easily comprehended, precisely since necessity reasons had dictated the architectural form that it had taken.

However, even if one takes into consideration all these facts, the general plan of the building still raises certain questions and queries. Attempts were made to give various solutions and interpretations to whatever did not satisfy the conception of archaeologists when they began studying it. Thus it was suggested by the German archaeologist Dörpfeld that the western section of the Erechtheion as seen today is unfinished. This theory was based on the fact that the northern porch extends further (westwards) than the extreme western wall, and on the other hand, that the Korai porch lies at the western end of the southern side. Dörpfeld believed that the western side continued further to the west, so that the Korai porch would be located in the centre of the southern side. This is a possible interpretation of course, which we cannot accept however, for it raises in turn further questions. Perhaps this incompleted plan, as it looks today, was due to what we have already said, i.e. to the cults which all had to be included in a single structure. Whatever the case may be, the Erechtheion with all the wealth and beauty of its ornaments provides an aesthetic pleasure to the visitor of our days, such as offered by the Ionic style.

After 1458 and the domination of the Turks, the Erechtheion was turned into a charem.

In front of the Erechtheion (further to the east) was the altar of Athena. The priests of the Parthenon as well as those of the Erechtheion, offered sacrifices there. Still further to the east was the sanctuary of Zeus Polieus where sacrifices were offered, the so - called « Bouphoneia », of which Pausanias, Aelianos, and other ancient writers speak. On the site where the Museum was later built, stood the sanctuary of Pandion.

These were then the main buildings on the Acropolis in Classical years and such remained the form of the sanctuary for a very long time. In the Roman period, at the time of Augustus, in front of the eastern side of the Parthenon a circular monopteral temple was erected in the Ionic style, clearly imitating the Erechtheion, in honour of Augustus and Rome.

Of the slopes of the Acropolis, it was possible to construct sanctuaries only on the southern one. Thus we have on that site, since the 5th century B.C., the odeum of Pericles and the temple of Dionysus, next to which the theatre was built; from the theatre however, we see the later phases today. On the same slope was also erected the sanctuary of Asklepios, whose cult was introduced in Attica around 420 B.C.; it comprised the temple, the sacred spring, and the «enkoimeterion», a long stoa where pilgrims spent the night, as encountered in all sanctuaries dedicated to the worship of Asklepios. In the years after Christ a Christian church was built on that site. In the second century B.C., southwards of the Asklepios sanctuary, was constructed the Stoa of Eumenes, named after the king of Pergamum Eumenes II, who erected it. The stoa had a length of 163 m. and a width of 17 m. Next to the Stoa of Eumenes (westwards) is the Odeum of Herodes Atticus, also named after its dedicator. It was built in A.D. 160, and the material used was marble. From this theatre are preserved today the wall of the skene, the great arches and the orchestra, as well as most of the seats.

In the following centuries the view from the Acropolis and from the foot of the hill changed, as we have already mentioned when describing the various buildings, according to the conquerors who came to Athens. Thus the area was altered, not only through the natural damages suffered by the buildings, but also through the various human interventions. A later plan, not applied however, was that of the architect Schinkel in 1832, who designed the palace of king Otto on the Acropolis, trying as much as possible to respect the ancient buildings. The fact that this plan was not realized has undoubtedly facilitated the systematic excavations and investigations carried out later on the entire site, which restored to the monuments the appearance they had before being changed by late alterations.

This brief survey of the Acropolis and the area around it, has allowed a quick glimpse into what has represented for centuries the great flourish and pure thought of the Classical era. What is most impressive is the fact that the most important monuments of art — not just Greek art — were produced precisely at the time when the fratricidal War between Greeks was in preparation. Even during the War and in the short intervals between it, construction activities did not cease on the Acropolis; during these intervals, as we have seen, the temple of Apteros Nike and the Erechtheion were built. Simultaneously there is an exceptional spiritual elevation through the writing of history by Herodotus and Thucydides and the development of tragedy rivalled by comedy. A new spur and direction is also given to philosophy. All these parallel movements produce a new form in art, the maturity witnessed in the creations of the 5th century B.C., which expresses the change that had taken place in the simple life of the Archaic period.

There is now a new way of looking at the world and a different conception of the problems of mankind. Perhaps the present-day visitors of the Acropolis can guess, or rather see, eventhough faintly, some of these things in the picture which confronts them when climbing on the rock as pilgrims.

1. Part of the Parthenon sekos and southern colonnade as seen from the North - East. The Doric columns are reflected on the floor of the sekos, wet from the rain.

2-3. View of the Acropolis from the South. The Odeum of Herodes Atticus and the long Stoa of Eumenes in the foreground; beyond the Stoa we can just discern the sanctuary of Asklepios.

4. The small Ionic temple of Wingless Victory as seen from the south wing of the Propylaea, which had no western wall.

5. Part of the central section of the Propylaea from the north-eastern angle. We can see two of the Doric columns of the western side, and another two Ionic columns of the inner colonnade. The capitals that would have supported the pedimental roof are missing from all the columns.

6. The temple of Athena Nike or Wingless Victory, from the North-East. It was erected on the bastion existing there since Mycenaean times. We can see the northern and eastern side of the temple, and an Ionic column of the western side. Part of the reliefs are still *in situ* on the frieze.

7. Ionic column from the inner colonnade of the central section of the Propylaea. It supports the roof, which consisted of carved panels, the cofferings, exquisitely ornamented with painted decoration.

8-9. Eastern side of the temple of Wingless Victory. On the facade there are four Ionic columns supporting the roof. On the frieze of this side there is a representation of the Assembly of the gods. The pediment is missing.

10.

11. From the south-eastern corner the figure of the Parthenon rises majestically with the Erechtheion on its left side.

12. The western and part of the northern side of the Parthenon as seen from the West. In the foreground, part of the architrave of the eastern side of the Propylaea.

13. The western side of the Parthenon as seen from the eastern porch of the Propylaea.

14-15. The Parthenon and the Erechtheion from the North - West. Part of the north-eastern side of the Propylaea can be seen on the right.

16-17. View of the Parthenon from the North-West. The great temple, which constituted an expression of the power and prosperity of Athens at the time of Pericles, was consecrated in 438 B.C. We can see part of the outer colonnade, the «pteron», as named in antiquity, from the northern and western side. The wall of the sekos is visible beyond the columns of the western side. The whole temple was erected on the surface of the ground on a three-stepped crepis.

18-19. From the western side of the Parthenon, behind the outer colonnade, we can see the celebrated frieze, a purely Ionic feature used for the first time in monumental form in a Doric temple. A large number of the frieze slabs has been preserved on the western side of the monument. At the left end, as we stand facing this side, we can see *in situ* the group of Cecrops with one of his daughters.

20. The sekos of the Parthenon surrounded by the northern and eastern colonnades. Mt. Lycabetus in the background. View from the South-West.

21. The Doric columns of the Parthenon are admired for their solid construction and fine fluting: they give one the impression that they may well carry the weight of the roof of the temple without bending (From the southern colonnade).

22-23. Part of the architrave on the southern side of the Parthenon is no longer in place. On a lower level we may see the temple of Olympian Zeus (Olympeion), whose construction had already begun in the 6th century B.C., at the time of Peisistratus.

24. The south-western corner of the Parthenon and the southern colonnade. View from the South-West.

25. The southern colonnade of the Parthenon, beyond which was the wall of the sekos. A passageway was thus formed between the wall and the colonnade.

26-27. The frieze of the Parthenon as preserved on the western side of the temple. We can see part of the Panathenaic procession with the line of young horsemen.

28-29. The Korai porch. The Korai are better known in our days as Caryatides. Four of them stand in a single line and another two are each behind those placed at either corner of the first row. The second from the left is in the British Museum; here we see its plaster reproduction.

30-31. The Korai were standing, the weight of their body resting on one leg; with their left hand they were slightly lifting their himation.

32. The Acropolis from the western side: in the foreground the temple of Athena Nike on the bastion, and the Propylaea; beyond them, the Parthenon emerges magnificently, while the Erechtheion appears on the left.

33. The eastern facade of the Parthenon. The outer colonnade of the pteron supporting the roof has been preserved. The pediment is almost entirely missing.

34. The south-eastern corner of the Erechtheion. Six Ionic columns were supporting the roof on the eastern side. At the western end of the southern wall we can see the « Caryatides» porch.

35b. The eastern side of the Erechtheion. The frieze in dark Eleusinian stone was decorated with marble statues almost carved in the round. Today we can only see the slab on which the statues had been fastened.

36-37. The Erechtheion from the West: we can see the southern side with the Korai porch at the western end, the western side, and the northern porch. Outside the western side was the open air sanctuary of Pandrosos with the sacred olive-tree of Athena. The Korai porch partly overlays the northern side of the « old temple» of Athena Polias, dated to the 6th century B.C., of which only the foundations have been preserved.

38-39. (Inv. No. 624). Among the first Archaic marble sculptures of the Acropolis is the «Moschophoros» (Calf-bearer), a mature man carrying a calf on his shoulders. It is dated earlier than the mid-6th century B.C., to 570-560 B.C. On the base of the statue there was an inscription with the name of the dedicator: Ρόμβος or Κρόμβος. The eyes were inserted.

40. (Inv. No. 4). A lioness attacking a bull: poros pediment from the eastern side of the Old Parthenon, forming the right part of the pediment; there should have been a corresponding representation on the left part. It is dated to the first decade of the 6th century B.C.

40. (Inv. No. 52). The «Pediment of the Olive». Also made of poros, it belongs to one of the small rectangular buildings which existed on the Acropolis in the 6th century B.C. It represents a building with peribolos on which can be seen an engraved olive-tree, after which the building had been named. In front of the peribolos and the building, parts of one male and three female figures have been preserved; only one of the female figures is fairly well preserved. This was probably a mythical representation after the myth of Achilles and Troïlos. Circa 580 B.C.

41-43. (Inv. No. 35). Poros pediment from the western side of the « old temple» of Athena Polias, situated southwards of the Erechtheion. On the left end of the pediment is depicted the struggle of Herakles and Triton, on the right the «Three-bodied demon», most probably Nereus, represented in the form of three bearded men whose torsoes rise from bodies of serpents; one is carrying a bird, the other a fire, and the third a representation of water. In the central part of the pediment archaeologists restore lions attacking a bull. Circa 570 B.C.

(Inv. No. 9). Poros pediment with representation of the « Deification of Herakles». It preserves the group of Zeus and Hera,

33

who are both depicted seated, Zeus on a throne, watching the procession, and Hera in frontal attitude; Iris, Herakles and Hermes are represented next. The statues are almot carved in the round. The painted decoration is partly preserved. Earlier than the mid-6th century B.C.

44. (Inv. No. 593). Headless statue of a Kore, dated before the mid-6th century B.C. She is dressed in a chiton and peplos with a himation over it. In her hands she holds a wreath and a pomegranate. A relief necklace is visible on her neck.

45. (Inv. No. 632). To the same date, i.e. shortly before the middle of the 6th century B.C., belongs the Sphinx whose front legs and back part of the body are missing. The Sphinxes, principally demonic creatures, formed the finials of funerary stelai.

46. (Inv. No. 606). Representation of a horse with rider. Only the front part of the horse's body and the rider's legs are preserved. Also preserved is the painted decoration on the rider's garment, from which we infer that the rider was wearing a Scythian or Persian dress. Dated to 520 B.C.

47. (Inv. No. 590). The head of the famous « Rampin Horseman ». The body of the horseman is exhibited in the Acropolis Museum, while the head is in the Louvre. In the Acropolis Museum we see the plaster reproduction of the head. The « Rampin Horseman » is the oldest statue of a rider in Archaic art, made before the mid-6th century B.C. A Kore — the « Peplophoros » — (Inv. No. 679) and a hunting hound (Inv. No. 143) are also attributed to the artist of the « Rampin Horseman »; both these works were made later than the Horseman.

48. (Inv. No. 143). A hunting hound has been preserved from Archaic times; it is depicted on the point of running. Circa 520 B.C. There should have been another such hound, as indicated by a fragment of a hound forming a pair with the first one.

49. (Inv. No. 700). Representation of a rider. From the horse are preserved only the body and one leg, from the rider only the legs. End of the 6th century B.C.

50. (Inv. No. 643). Head of a Kore dated to the end of the 6th century B.C., circa 510 B.C. One of the finest works of Archaic sculpture, undoubtedly the work of a great artist.

51. (Inv. No. 625). The Athena of Endoios. Headless statue of the goddess Athena attributed to the artist Endoios. The goddess is represented seated. The locks of her hair fall on her shoulders. On the chest is the aegis with the gorgoneion in the centre. The right leg of the goddess is placed backwards of the left. Dated to circa 530 B.C.

34

52-53. (Inv. No. 679). The « Peplophoros » is one of the most remarkable statues of Korai, among the earliest of its kind, dated to circa 540-530 B.C. She is dressed in an Ionic chiton with an Attic peplos over it, falling without any folds. A small part of the painted decorarion of her dress is still visible today.

54-55. (Inv. No. 673). This Kore, who is attributed, according to some archaeologists, to the artist of Aristodikos, is dated to 520 B.C. She is wearing a chiton and himation.

56-57. (Inv. No. 675). Colours are fairly well preserved on this Kore, so that it gives a picture of the polychromy of ancient statues. The work is probably Cycladic.

58-59. (Inv. No. 671). In the last quarter of the 6th century B.C., the peplos no longer formed part of women's garments, as we can see in this Kore. The chiton and himation fall on the figure without excessively rich folds.

60-61. (Inv. No. 680). One of the best preserved statues of Korai. Even the extreme parts of the hands are preserved, which is very rare in these statues. She is holding a fruit in her left hand. Her hair is abundantly falling on her chest. Circa 520-510 B.C.

62. (Inv. No. 681). Statue of a Kore attributed to the artist Antenor, according to the inscription on a base, which is considered to have probably belonged to the statue. Nearchos is cited as the dedicator. The eyes were inserted. The himation falls in rich folds on the body, while the chiton is slightly lifted with the left hand. Traces of fire are clearly visible on the statue.

64-65. (Inv. No. 670). Statue of a Kore dressed only in a chiton which is girded. With the left hand, adorned with a bracelet, she holds part of the cloth falling between the legs. The painted decoration is still preserved. Dated to 520-510 B.C.

66-67. (Inv. No. 674). One of the best statues of Korai is dated shortly before 500 B.C. A striking feature on her face are her eyes, which have an upward slant, while the whole face has an expression of seriousness.

68-69. (Inv. No. 684). Statue of a Kore dated to the beginnings of the 5th century B.C. We notice on the face a horizontal line in the eyes and the mouth, and a stylization in the garment.

70-71. (Inv. No. 682). Statue of a Kore belonging to the last quarter of the 6th century B.C. We note a new expression on the features of the face and great elaboration in the hair style. With the left hand she was lifting the chiton. The painted decoration was also rich.

72. (Inv, No, 688). The « Propylaea Kore » already belongs to the

Classical period, as we may see from the expression on the face and from the dress, which falls on the body without the rich drapery of the Archaic Korai. Circa 480 B.C.

73. (Inv. No. 686). A Kore statue has survived since the beginnings of the 5th century B.C.,; named after the dedicator who offered her, she is known as the « Kore of Euthydikos ». The name of the dedicator is inscribed on the base of the statue. The torso of the statue is cylindrical and the flesh is discerned through the outline of the dress. The features of the face are heavy, the garment more plain. It is considered as the last of the Archaic Korai. Circa 490-480 B.C.

74-75. (Inv. No. 695). Relief belonging to the period of the « austere style ». It represents the « Mourning Athena », and is dated to 460-450 B.C. The goddess leans with her left hand on the lance while her right hand rests on her hip. One leg is in a completely relaxed position, only the toes are touching the ground. The head is slightly inclined downwards: the goddess is contemplating a stele set up in front of her. She is wearing the Doric peplos.

76. (Inv. No. 689). Head of the « Blond ephebos », who was given that name because of the colour existing on his hair when it was found. He has a splendid serious and somewhat distracted expression. The head was inclined towards the right shoulder. The hair was falling on the forehead and the temples; at the back it was forming two braids which were covered in front by the locks of the forehead. The work had been considered as Peloponnesian, but this is not certain. Dated to 480 B.C.

77. (Inv. No. 698). Statue of a nude ephebos known as the « Kritios boy» because of the similarity of his torso and head to the group of the Tyrannicides by Kritios and Nesiotis. He rests his weight on the left leg and his head is slightly turned to the right. The statue has a Classical structure; the proportions of the body are different from those of the Archaic statues. The eyes were inserted, and the hair was turned inwards at the base of the head. Circa 480 B.C.

78-79. (Inv. No. 856). From the eastern side of the Parthenon frieze, we may see here one of the finest slabs depicting the Assembly of gods. The gods, facing right, are represented seated: Poseidon, to whom Apollo, the Delphic god, turns; the latter is dressed in a himation covering his left shoulder and rests his feet on a stool. Next are Artemis and part of the very damaged figure of Aphrodite. The figures, which have a Classical structure in the construction of their body and face, are ascribed to Alcamenes, the pupil of Pheidias.

80-81. (Inv. No. 864). The procession of youths leading the sacrificial animals was followed by others carrying various objects. On this slab which belonged to the frieze on the northern side of the Parthenon, we see three youths carrying hydriai on their shoulders, while a fourth one is bending and also carrying a hydria. The figures are dressed in himatia covering their left shoulder, and proceed with a serious expression on their faces. At the right end of the slab is preserved part of a male figure holding a flute in his hand. The figure belongs to the group of musicians coming next.

82. (Inv. No. 862). Riding youths facing left. One of them looks backwards, while his companion coming next raises his right hand and places it on his head. The figures are not in array, but are grouped in the foreground and background (Frieze slab from the northern side).

83. (Inv. No. 863). On the northern frieze, the scene was continued with the riding youths. Here we see the horsemen facing left and a taxinomos among them facing right; he is the only one wearing a long himation. The movement of the horses is remarkable.

84. (Inv. No. 860). A procession of youths facing left, leading the sacrificial rams. We see a detail from this scene, with a youth looking backwards, most probably talking to another youth who comes next. A ram walks in front of the figure (Northern frieze).

85. (Inv. No. 973). Slab from the parapet of the temple of Wingless Victory, bearing a representation of a Nike who unties her sandal. She bends forwards and lifts her right leg, while rich and exquisite folds are formed at the back of her body. The parapet, as attested by the technique of the reliefs, was made in the end of the 5th century B.C., circa 408 B.C. (Acropolis Museum).

86. (Inv. No. 1331). Portrait of Alexander the Great, an original work of a great artist of the end of the 4th century B.C. The features of the portrait are idealized.

87. (Inv. No. 1313). Portrait of a philosopher of the late antiquity. He wears a wreath on his head. Dated to 430 A.D.

Key Plan
for the

MODEL OF THE ACROPOLIS OF ATHENS

by

Gorham Phillips Stevens

PLAN REPÈRE

DE LA

MAQUETTE DE L' ACROPOLE D' ATHÈNES

par

Gorham Phillips Stevens

PLAN REPÈRE

DE LA

MODEL OF THE ACROPOLIS OF ATHENS   MAQUETTE DE L' ACROPOLE D' ATHÈNES   DER AKROPOLIS VON ATHEN

von

Gorham Phillips Stevens

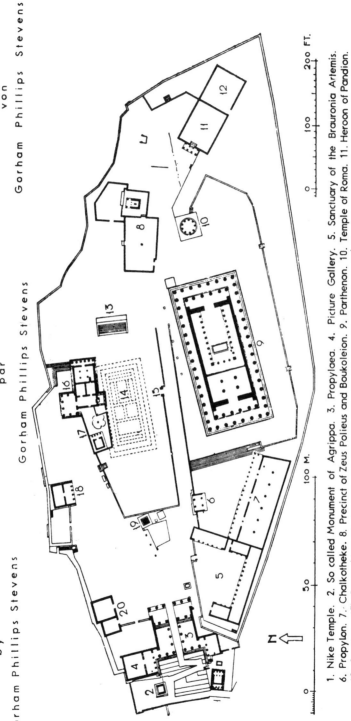

1. Nike Temple. 2. So called Monument of Agrippa. 3. Propylaea. 4. Picture Gallery. 5. Sanctuary of the Brauronia Artemis.
6. Propylon. 7. Chalkotheke. 8. Precinct of Zeus Polieus and Boukoleion. 9. Parthenon. 10. Temple of Roma. 11. Heroon of Pandion.
12. Service. 13. Great Altar of Athena. 14. Old Temple of Athena. 15. Propylon. 16. Erechtheum. 17. Pandroseum, Temple of
Pandrosus, Sacred Olive Tree, Cecropium. 18. Dwelling of the Arrephori. 19. Promachos. 20. Service Building. (?)

1. Temple de la Victoire et 2. Monument dit d' Aprippa 3. Propylées 4. Gallerie de Tableaux 5. Sanctuaire d' Artemis Brauronienne.
6. Propylon 7. Chalkotheke. 8. District de Zeus Polieus et Boukoleion 9. Parthénon. 10. Temple de Rome. 11. Heroon de Pandion
12. Service. 13. Grand Autel d' Athéna. 14. Ancien Temple d' Athéna. 15. Propylon. 16. Erechthéion 17. Pandrosseion, Temple de
Pandrosse, Olivier Sacré, Cecropeion. 18. Demeure des Arrephori. 19. Promachos. 20. Edifice de Service.

1. Nike Tempel. 2. Das Sogenanntes Agrippa-Denkmal. 3. Propyläen. 4. Gemäldegalerie. 5. Heiligtum der Wrauronischen Artemis. 6. Propylon. 7. Chalkotheke. 8. Heiligtum des Zeus Polieus und Boukoleion. 9. Parthenon. 10. Tempel von Rom. 11. Herroon
von Pandion. 12. Bedienungsgebäude. 13. Grosser Athene-Altar. 14. Antiker Athene-Tempel. 15. Propylon. 16. Erechtheion.

slab which belonged to the frieze on the northern side of the Parthenon, we see three youths carrying hydriai on their shoulders, while a fourth one is bending and also carrying a hydria. The figures are dressed in himatia covering their left shoulder, and proceed with a serious expression on their faces. At the right end of the slab is preserved part of a male figure holding a flute in his hand. The figure belongs to the group of musicians coming next.

82. (Inv. No. 862). Riding youths facing left. One of them looks backwards, while his companion coming next raises his right hand and places it on his head. The figures are not in array, but are grouped in the foreground and background (Frieze slab from the northern side).

83. (Inv. No. 863). On the northern frieze, the scene was continued with the riding youths. Here we see the horsemen facing left and a taxinomos among them facing right; he is the only one wearing a long himation. The movement of the horses is remarkable.

84. (Inv. No. 860). A procession of youths facing left, leading the sacrificial rams. We see a detail from this scene, with a youth looking backwards, most probably talking to another youth who comes next. A ram walks in front of the figure (Northern frieze).

85. (Inv. No. 973). Slab from the parapet of the temple of Wingless Victory, bearing a representation of a Nike who unties her sandal. She bends forwards and lifts her right leg, while rich and exquisite folds are formed at the back of her body. The parapet, as attested by the technique of the reliefs, was made in the end of the 5th century B.C., circa 408 B.C. (Acropolis Museum).

86. (Inv. No. 1331). Portrait of Alexander the Great, an original work of a great artist of the end of the 4th century B.C. The features of the portrait are idealized.

87. (Inv. No. 1313). Portrait of a philosopher of the late antiquity. He wears a wreath on his head. Dated to 430 A.D.

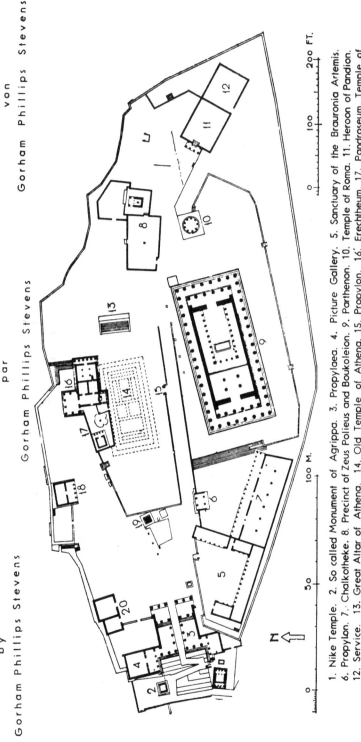

PLAN REPÉRE

DE LA

MAQUETTE DE L' ACROPOLE D' ATHÉNES

par

Gorham Phillips Stevens

Key Plan

for the

MODEL OF THE ACROPOLIS OF ATHENS

by

Gorham Phillips Stevens

DER AKROPOLIS VON ATHEN

von

Gorham Phillips Stevens

1. Nike Temple. 2. So called Monument of Agrippa. 3. Propylaea. 4. Picture Gallery. 5. Sanctuary of the Brauronia Artemis. 6. Propylon. 7. Chalkotheke. 8. Precinct of Zeus Polieus and Boukoleion. 9. Parthenon. 10. Temple of Roma. 11. Heroon of Pandion. 12. Service. 13. Great Altar of Athena. 14. Old Temple of Athena. 15. Propylon. 16. Erechtheum. 17. Pandroseum, Temple of Pandrosus, Sacred Olive Tree, Cecropium. 18. Dwelling of the Arrephori. 19. Promachos. 20. Service Building. (?)

1. Temple de la Victoir et 2. Monument dit d' Aprippa 3. Propylées 4. Gallerie de Tableaux 5. Sanctuaire d' Artemis Brauronienne. 6. Propylon 7. Chalkotheke. 8. District de Zeus Polieus et Boukoleion 9. Parthénon. 10. Temple de Rome. 11. Heroon de Pandion 12. Service. 13. Grand Autel d' Athéna. 14. Ancien Temple d' Athéna. 15. Propylon. 16. Erechthéion 17. Pandrosseion, Temple de Pandrosse, Olivier Sacré, Cecropeion. 18. Demeure des Arrephori. 19. Promachos. 20. Edifice de Service.

1. Nike Tempel. 2. Das Sogenanntes Agrippa-Denkmal. 3. Propyläen. 4. Gemäldegalerie. 5. Heiligtum der Wrauronischen Artemis. 6. Propylon. 7. Chalkotheke. 8. Heiligtum des Zeus Polieus und Boukoleion. 9. Parthenon. 10. Tempel von Rom. 11. Herroon von Pandion. 12. Bedienungsgebäude. 13. Grosser Athene-Altar. 14. Antiker Athene-Tempel. 15. Propylon. 16. Erechtheion.

5

ΑΠΑΓΟΡΕΥΕΤΑΙ Η ΔΙΑΒΑΣΙΣ
ΚΙΝΔΥΝΟΣ
PASSAGE FORBIDDEN
DANGER

13

25

(Inv. No. 624)

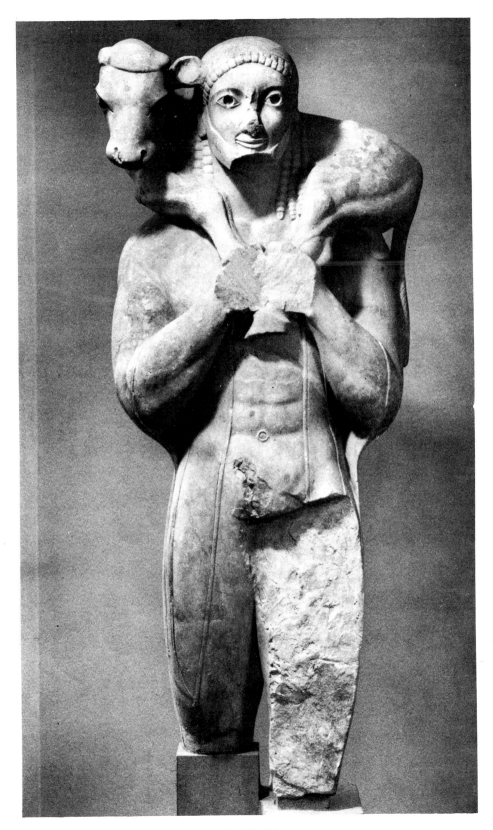

(Inv. No. 624)

(Inv. No. 4)

(Inv. No. 52)

(Inv. No. 35)

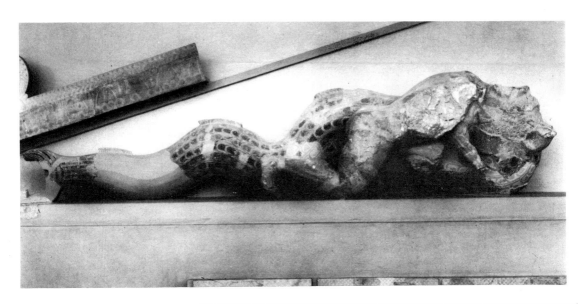

(Inv. No. 35)

(Inv. No. 9)

(Inv. No. 593)

(Inv. No. 632)

(Inv. No. 606)

(Inv. No. 590)

(Inv. No. 143)

(Inv. No. 700)

(Inv. No 643)

(Inv. No. 625)

(Inv. No. 679)

(Inv. No. 679)

(Inv. No. 673)

(Inv. No. 673)

(Inv. No. 671)

(Inv. No. 671)

(Inv. No. 680)

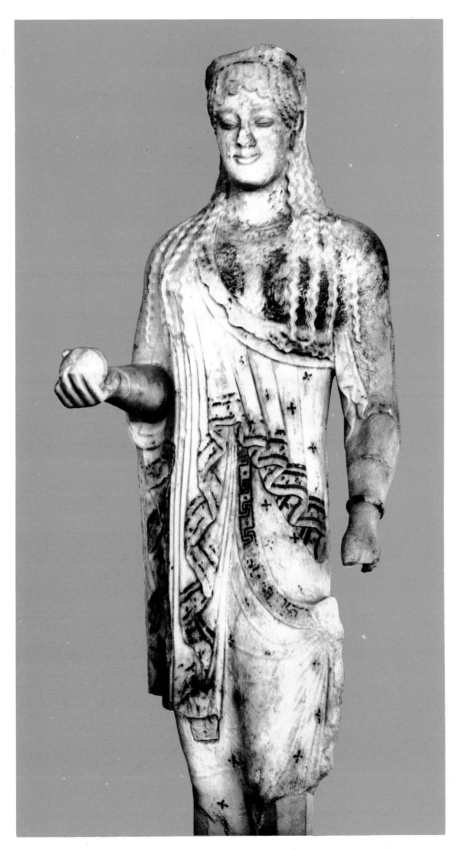

61

(Inv. No. 681

(Inv. No. 670)

(Inv. No. 670)

(Inv. No. 674)

(Inv. No. 674)

(Inv. No. 684)

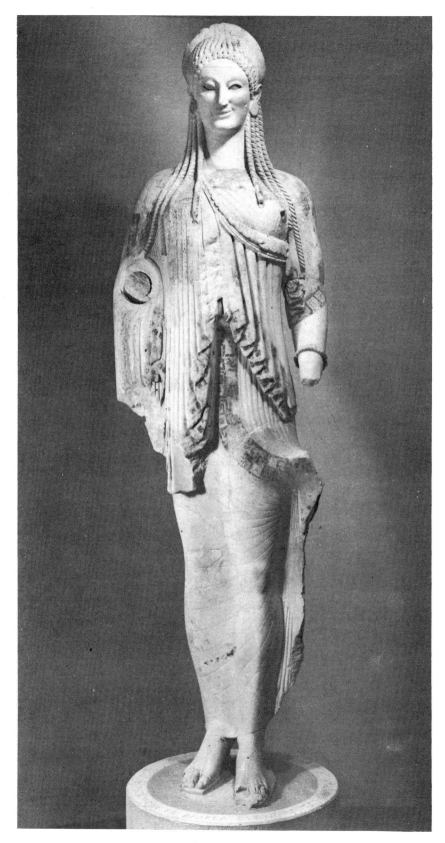

(Inv. No. 682)

(Inv. Do. 688)

(Inv. No. 686)

(Inv. No. 695)

(Inv. No. 695)

(Inv. No. 689)

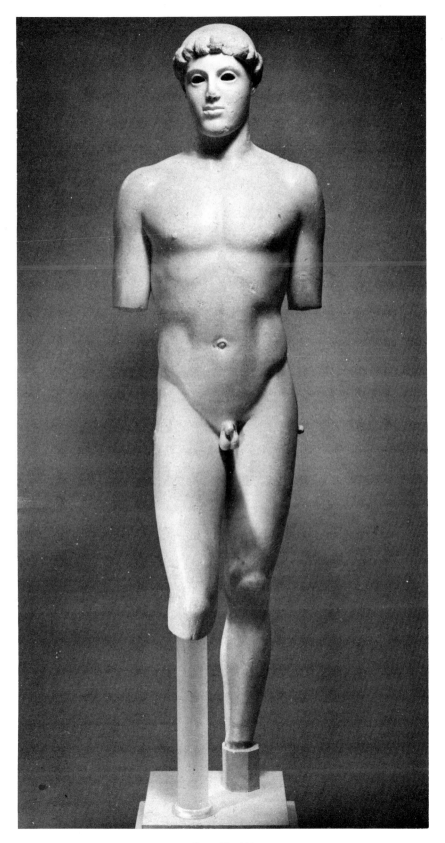

(Inv. No. 856)

(Inv. No. 856)

(Inv. No. 864)

(Inv. No. 862)

(Inv. No. 863)

(Inv. No. 860)

(Inv. No. 973)

(Inv. No. 1331)